Android Certification Preparation Guide with Practice Test

Preparation Questions and Answers for Certification
Exam Code: AND-401

Information
Technology
Education
Academy

DEDICATION

I would like to thank all my colleagues and family for support.

QUESTION 1
What Activity method you would use to retrieve a reference to an Android view by using the id attribute of a resource XML?

A. findViewByReference(int id) B. findViewById(int id)
C. retrieveResourceById(int id) D. findViewById(String id)

Correct Answer: B Section: (none) Explanation

Explanation/Reference:

QUESTION 2
What does the following line of code achieve?
Intent intent = new Intent(FirstActivity.this, SecondActivity.class);

A. Creates a hidden Intent. B. Creates an implicit Intent. C. Create an explicit Intent. D. Starts an activity.

Correct Answer: C Section: (none) Explanation

Explanation/Reference: QUESTION 3

Which of the following is NOT a valid usage of Intents?

A. Activate and Activity. B. Activate a Service.
C. Activate a Broadcast receiver.
D. Activate a SQLite DB Connection.

Correct Answer: D Section: (none) Explanation

Explanation/Reference:

QUESTION 4
Which of the following is not a valid Android resource file name?

A. mylayout.xml B. myLayout.xml C. my_layout.xml D. mylayout1.xml

Correct Answer: B Section: (none) Explanation

Explanation/Reference:

QUESTION 5
What is a correct statement about XML layout file?

A. layout PNG image file.
B. A layout defines the visual structure for a user interface, such as the UI for an activity or app widget. C. A file that contains all application permission information.
D. A file that contains a single activity widget.

Correct Answer: B
Section: (none)
Explanation

Explanation/Reference:

QUESTION 6
Which folder contains the Android project Java files?

A. res
B. manifests
C. assets
D. java

Correct Answer: D Section: (none) Explanation

Explanation/Reference:

QUESTION 7
Which of the following files specifies the minimum required Android SDK version your application supports?

A. main.xml
B. R.java
C. strings.xml
D. build.gradle

Correct Answer: D Section: (none) Explanation

Explanation/Reference:

QUESTION 8
What is the name of the class used by Intent to store additional information?

A. Extra

B. Parcelable
C. Bundle
D. DataStore

Correct Answer: C Section: (none) Explanation

Explanation/Reference:

QUESTION 9
Which of the following is not included in the Android application framework?.

A. WindowManager
B. NotificationManager
C. DialerManager
D. PackageManager

Correct Answer: C Section: (none) Explanation

Explanation/Reference:

QUESTION 10
Which of the following is NOT true about the R.java file?

A. It is auto-generated during the build of the project.
B. It is used by developers to access any resource through an ID.
C. It can be modified manually to change the ID of a resource.
D. It contains resource IDs for all resources in your /res/ folder.

Correct Answer: C Section: (none) Explanation

Explanation/Reference:

QUESTION 11
You can create a custom view by extending class Activity.

A. True B. False C.
D.

Correct Answer: B Section: (none) Explanation

Explanation/Reference:

QUESTION 12
Which of these files contains text values that you can use in your application?

A. AndroidManifest.xml
B. res/Text.xml
C. res/layout/Main.xml
D. res/values/strings.xml

Correct Answer: D Section: (none) Explanation

Explanation/Reference:

QUESTION 13
What does the Android project folder "res/" contain?

A. Java Activity classes
B. Resource files
C. Java source code
D. Libraries

Correct Answer: B Section: (none) Explanation

Explanation/Reference:

QUESTION 14
What does this code do? Intent intent = new Intent( );
intent.setAction(Intent.ACTION_VIEW);
intent.setData(android.net.Uri.parse("http://www.androidatc.com"
));
startActivity(intent);

A. Starts a sub-activity. B. Starts a service.
C. Sends results to another activity.
D. Starts an activity using an implicit intent.

Correct Answer: D Section: (none) Explanation

Explanation/Reference:

QUESTION 15
Which of the following is a Java call-back method invoked when a view is clicked?

A. Detector
B. All answers are correct
C. OnClickDetector
D. OnClickListener

Correct Answer: D Section: (none) Explanation

Explanation/Reference:

QUESTION 16
Which of the following is NOT an Activity lifecycle call-back method?

A. onStart
B. onCreate
C. onPause
D. onBackPressed

Correct Answer: D Section: (none) Explanation

Explanation/Reference:

QUESTION 17
Which of the following methods is used to close an activity?

A. Destroy( ) B. Finish( ) C. Stop( )
D. Close( )

QUESTION 18
Which of the following Activity life-cycle methods is called once the activity is no longer visible?

A. onOnce B. onPause C. onDestroy D. onHide

QUESTION 19
Which of the following is a correct Android Manifest statement?

A. <uses-permission android:name ="android.Internet"/>
B. <uses-permission android:name ="android.Internet"></uses-permission> C. <uses-permission android:name ="android.permission.Internet">
D. <uses-permission android:name ="android.permission.Internet"/>

QUESTION 20
Which of the following is true about attribute android:windowSoftInputMode of the <activity> tag in file AndroidManifest.xml?

A. It specifies whether the window is in full screen or not.
B. It adjusts how the main window of the activity interacts with keyboard. C. It adjusts how the window should be launched.
D. It adjusts the window orientation.

QUESTION 21
Which of the following tools dumps system log messages including stack traces when the device or emulator throws an error?

A. DDMS B. Logcat C. Console D. ADB

Correct Answer: B Section: (none) Explanation

Explanation/Reference:

QUESTION 22
JavaScript is enabled by default in a WebView.

A. True
B. False

Correct Answer: B Section: (none) Explanation

Explanation/Reference:

QUESTION 23
Which of the following lines of code enables JavaScript in WebView?

A. myWebView.setJavaScriptEnabled(true);
B. myWebView.getJavaScriptSettings.setEnabled(true);
C. myWebView.getSettings().setJavaScriptEnabled(true);
 D. Java script is always enabled in WebView

Correct Answer: C Section: (none) Explanation

Explanation/Reference:

QUESTION 24
What two methods you have to override when implementing Android context menus?

A. onCreateOptionsMenu, onCreateContextMenu B.
onCreateContextMenu, onContextItemSelected C.
onCreateOptionsMenu, onOptionsItemSelected D.
onCreateOptionsMenu, onContextItemSelected

Correct Answer: B Section: (none) Explanation

Explanation/Reference:

QUESTION 25
What two methods you have to override when implementing
Android option menus?

A. onCreateOptionsMenu, onCreateContextMenu B.
onCreateContextMenu, onContextItemSelected C.
onCreateOptionsMenu, onOptionsItemSelected D.
onCreateOptionsMenu, onContextItemSelected

Correct Answer: C Section: (none) Explanation

Explanation/Reference:

QUESTION 26
Which of the following is a call-back method that inflates an
options menu from file res/menu/menu.xml?

A. onOptionsItemSelected
B. onCreate
C. onCreateMenu
D. onCreateOptionsMenu

Correct Answer: D Section: (none) Explanation

Explanation/Reference:

QUESTION 27
Which of the following Activity methods is invoked when the user
clicks on an options menu item?

A. onItemClicked
B. onItemSelected
C. onOptionsItemClicked
D. onOptionsItemSelected

Correct Answer: D Section: (none) Explanation

Explanation/Reference:

QUESTION 28
Which of the following WebView methods allows you to manually load HTML from String variable?

A. loadData
B. loadHTML

C. loadCustomData
D. loadCustomHTML

Correct Answer: A Section: (none) Explanation

Explanation/Reference:

QUESTION 29
Which of the following is the base class of all layout UI widgets?

A. ListView B. Layout C. View
D. ViewGroup

Correct Answer: C Section: (none) Explanation

Explanation/Reference:

QUESTION 30
Which of the following is NOT a correct constructer for ArrayAdapter?

A. ArrayAdapter(Context context)
B. ArrayAdapter (Context context, int recourse)

C. ArrayAdpater (Context context , int resource, int textViewResourceId) D. ArrayAdapter (Context context , int resource, List<T> items)

Correct Answer: A Section: (none) Explanation

Explanation/Reference:

QUESTION 31
Which of the following adds a click listener to items in a listView?

A. setonClickListener
B. setonItemClickListener
C. setonItemClicked
D. setonListItemClickListener

Correct Answer: B Section: (none) Explanation

Explanation/Reference:

QUESTION 32
Which of the following makes a ListView Clickable?

A. setClickable(true)
B. setVisibility(View.Visible)
C. setEnabled(true)
D. setItemsEnabled(true)

Correct Answer: C Section: (none) Explanation

Explanation/Reference:

QUESTION 33
Which of the following is true about implicit intents? (Choose two)

A. They do not have a component specified.
B. They have components specified to run an exact class.
C. They must include information that allows Android system to know which Android components able to catch the intent. D. They must contain extra information saved in a Bundle object.

QUESTION 34

An AsyncTask can be cancelled anytime from any thread.

A. True B. False C.
D.

QUESTION 35

Which of the following is NOT true about onMeasure( ) method of class View?

A. It measures the view and its contents to determine the measured width and height. B. It is invoked by measure( ).
C. The When overriding this method, a developer must call setMeasuredDimension( ). D. It takes three parameters: the height, width, and the depth of the view.

QUESTION 36

Which of the following Activity life-cycle methods is invoked first when another activity is shown?

A. onPause( ) B. onCreate( ) C. onStop( )
D. onDestroy( )

QUESTION 37

Which version of Android Studio introduced the "Instant Run" feature?

A. 1.4
B. 1.5
C. 2.0
D. 2.2

Correct Answer: C Section: (none) Explanation

Explanation/Reference:

QUESTION 38
What is the minimum Android SDK version required for using "Instant Run" feature of Android Studio?

A. 15
B. 19
C. 21
D. 23

Correct Answer: A Section: (none) Explanation

Explanation/Reference:

QUESTION 39
Which of following is NOT correct about Battery Historian tool?

A. It is an open source script.
B. It converts the battery data collected by Batterystats into HTML visualization. C. It collects and converts the battery data into HTML visualization.
D. It is not the part of Android framework.

Correct Answer: C Section: (none) Explanation

Explanation/Reference:

QUESTION 40

Which of the following is NOT the primary hardware involved performing simple task like putting pixels on screen?

A. CPU B. GPU
C. Memory storage
D. Cache

Correct Answer: D Section: (none) Explanation

Explanation/Reference: QUESTION 41

Which of the following is required for getting the best output from performance profiling tools in Android Studio?

A. It works only on real devices.
B. Disable the instant run before profiling the app. C. Enable the instant run before profiling the app.
D. It works only on real devices and enable the instant run before profiling the app.

Correct Answer: D Section: (none) Explanation

Explanation/Reference:

QUESTION 42
Which of the following make RecyclerView a better option to use for larger data sets?

A. Layout Managers for positioning items.
B. Default animations for adding and removing list items. C. Reuse the item views when they are no longer visible. D. All answers are correct

Correct Answer: D Section: (none) Explanation

Explanation/Reference:

QUESTION 43
Which of the following is NOT correct about RecyclerView?

A. Adapter is not needed in RecyclerView. B. It is more efficient than ListView.
C. It eliminates the need of use of ViewHolder.
D. "Adapter is not needed in RecyclerView" and "It eliminates the need of use of ViewHolder ".

Correct Answer: D
Section: (none)
Explanation

Explanation/Reference:

QUESTION 44
CardView extends from which of the following:

A. RelativeLayout B. LinearLayout C. TableLayout
D. FrameLayout

Correct Answer: D Section: (none) Explanation

Explanation/Reference:

QUESTION 45
In which Android version Runtime permissions were added?

A. Android 4.4
B. Android 5.0
C. Android 6.0
D. Android 5.1

Correct Answer: C Section: (none) Explanation

Explanation/Reference:

QUESTION 46
Which of the following are NOT types of Runtime permission? (Choose two)

A. Normal Permissions.

B. Negative Permissions.

C. Dangerous Permissions. D. Essential Permissions.

Correct Answer: BD Section: (none) Explanation

Explanation/Reference:

QUESTION 47
Which of the following is NOT correct about deep linking?

A. It enables Google to crawl your app content.
B. It allows users to enter your app from search results.
C. You have to add intent filters in activities tags in
AndroidManifest. D. You add intent filter in application tag in
AndroidManifest.

Correct Answer: D Section: (none) Explanation

Explanation/Reference:

QUESTION 48
Which of the following tags is not added in <intent-filter> for
enabling deep linking in your application?

A. <data>
B. <category>
 C. <url>
D. <action>

Correct Answer: C Section: (none) Explanation

Explanation/Reference:

QUESTION 49
Which of the following options are true for ConstraintLayout?

A. It is available in API level 21 and above. B. It is available in
API level 24 and above. C. It is available in API level 9 and
above. D. All answers are incorrect.

Correct Answer: C Section: (none) Explanation

QUESTION 50
What existing layout is closest to ConstraintLayout in terms of functionality?

A. LinearLayout B. FrameLayout C. GridLayout
D. All answers are incorrect

Correct Answer: D Section: (none) Explanation

Explanation/Reference:

QUESTION 51
Which Method allows setting action to snackbars?

A. setCallback(view)
B. setAction(CharSequence,View) C. setOnClickListener( )
D. It is not allowed

Correct Answer: B Section: (none) Explanation

Explanation/Reference:

QUESTION 52
How is the lifecycle of Service connected to the component that started it?

A. Same Lifecycler
B. Parallel Lifecycle
C. Sequence Lifecycle
D. Independent

Correct Answer: D Section: (none) Explanation

Explanation/Reference:

QUESTION 53

What work is suitable for Android Services?

A. Networking Operations. B. Streaming.
C. Updating Widgets.
D. All answers are correct.

Correct Answer: D Section: (none) Explanation

Explanation/Reference:

QUESTION 54
How can we register broadcast receiver?

A. In the Manifest file.
B. By calling Context.registerReceiver( ) method. C. From a
layout definition file.
D. In the Manifest file or by calling Context.registerReceiver( )
method.

Correct Answer: D Section: (none) Explanation

Explanation/Reference:

QUESTION 55
Which of the following is used to group messages in bundled
notifications?

A. Topic
B. Title
C. Subject
D. Tag

Correct Answer: A Section: (none) Explanation

Explanation/Reference:

QUESTION 56
What is direct reply in Android 7 ?

A. Feature that automatically replies using AI. B. Feature that shows reply suggestions.

C. Gives ability to reply from notification of Android. D. Helps manage system message replies.

Correct Answer: C Section: (none) Explanation

Explanation/Reference:

QUESTION 57
Which of the following are constants for Location providers?

A. LocationManager.GPS_PROVIDER and LocationManager.NETWORK_PROVIDER. B. LocationManager.GPS_PROVIDER and LocationManager.GMS_PROVIDER.
C. LocationManager.GMS_PROVIDER and LocationManager.GPS_PROVIDER. D. LocationManager.GPS_PROVIDER and LocationManager.GCM_PROVIDER.

Correct Answer: A Section: (none) Explanation

Explanation/Reference:

QUESTION 58
Best practice to implement Google Maps is to use Webview that calls the online Google Map API.

A. True
B. False

Correct Answer: B Section: (none) Explanation

Explanation/Reference:

QUESTION 59
Which of the following permission is necessary for capturing geo-coordinates?

A. android.permission.ACCESS_LOCATION
B. android.permission.ACCESS_LOCATION_FINE
C. android.permission.ACCESS_FINE_LOCATION
D. All answers are incorrect

Correct Answer: C Section: (none) Explanation

Explanation/Reference:

QUESTION 60
GPS provider requires a physical device and cannot be tested on an Emulator.

A. True
B. False

Correct Answer: B Section: (none) Explanation

Explanation/Reference:

QUESTION 61
What does the following code achieve?
Intent intent = new Intent(FirstActivity.this, SecondActivity.class);
startActivityForResult(intent);

A. Starts a browser activity
B. Starts a sub-activity
C. Starts an activity service

D. Sends results to another activity

Correct Answer: B Section: (none) Explanation

Explanation/Reference:

QUESTION 62
When using an implicit intent, what process does the system use to know what to do with it?

A. Intent resolution B. Intent declaration C. Intent overloading D. Intent transition

Correct Answer: A **Section: (none) Explanation**

Explanation/Reference:

QUESTION 63
Which of the following is NOT true about the MenuItem interface?

A. The MenuItem instance will be returned by the Menu class add(...) method. B. MenuItem can decide the Intent issued when clicking menu components.
C. MenuItem can display either an icon or text. D. MenuItem can set a checkbox.

Correct Answer: B **Section: (none) Explanation**

Explanation/Reference:

QUESTION 64

Which of the following is correct about application file access in the Android system?

A. Generally, files are handled as dedicated resources per each application.
B. Files created by an application can be directly accessed by any application.
C. The content of a file created by an application cannot be accessed by any other application. D. You can only access a file from within an Activity.

Correct Answer: A **Section: (none) Explanation**

Explanation/Reference:

QUESTION 65

Which of following is incorrect about the Toast class?

A. You can set a custom layout for a Toast
B. A Toast can only by created by an Activity class
C. There is no need to close or hide a Toast, since it closes automatically
D. A Toast is displayed for only one of the following periods: Toast.LENGHT_SHORT or Toast.LENGTH_LONG

Correct Answer: B Section: (none) Explanation

Explanation/Reference:

QUESTION 66
Which of the following does not have a ContentProvider component provided natively by Android SDK?

A. The contacts list
B. The telephone log
C. The bookmarks
D. The application list

Correct Answer: D
Section: (none)
Explanation

Explanation/Reference:

QUESTION 67
When creating a file using android.content.Context.openFileOutput("test.txt", 0), where is the file created?

A. /data/app/<package name>/files
B. /data/data/<package name>/files
C. /system/app/<package name>/files
D. Application /system/data/<package name>/files

Correct Answer: B Section: (none) Explanation

Explanation/Reference:

QUESTION 68
Which of the following is incorrect about the LogCat tool?

A. A LogCat UI tool is available inside Android Studio.
B. You can create a log in your application using Log.v(String,
String). C. Each log message has a tag.
D. Only one class of your applications can create log entries, and
it should be component class (Activity, Service,...etc).

Correct Answer: D Section: (none) Explanation

Explanation/Reference:

QUESTION 69
Which of the following information cannot be included in the
Manifest file?

A. The activities contained in the application.

B. The permissions required by the application.
C. The application's minimum SDK version required.
D. The handset models compatible with your application.

Correct Answer: D Section: (none) Explanation

Explanation/Reference:

QUESTION 70
Which method should you use to start a sub-activity?

A. startActivity(Intent intent)
B. startActivityForResult(Intent intent , int requestCode) C.
startService(Intent intent)
D. startSubActivity(Intent intent)

Correct Answer: B Section: (none) Explanation

Explanation/Reference:
QUESTION 71

Which of the following tools creates certificates for signing Android applications?

A. adb
B. logcat C. keytool D. certgen

Correct Answer: C Section: (none) Explanation

Explanation/Reference:

QUESTION 72
Which Android permission you should add to allow your application to read the device's address book?

A. READ_ADDRESS_DATA B. READ_PHONE_STATE
C. READ_PHONE_CONTACTS D. READ_CONTACTS

Correct Answer: D Section: (none) Explanation

Explanation/Reference:

QUESTION 73
In which Activity life-cycle method you should do all of your normal static set up such as: creating views and bind data to lists?

A. onResume( ) B. onStart( )
C. onCreate( ) D. onPause( )

Correct Answer: C Section: (none) Explanation

Explanation/Reference:

QUESTION 74
Which of the following lines of code starts activity Activity2 from a current activity Activity1?

A. Intent intent = new Intent(this,new Activity2());
                    startActivity(intent);
B. Intent intent = new Intent(new Activity2());
                    startActivity(intent);

C. Intent intent = new Intent (Activity1.class,Activity2.class);
                    startActivity(intent);
D. Intent intent = new Intent(this,Activity2.class);
                    startActivity(intent);

Correct Answer: D Section: (none) Explanation

Explanation/Reference:

QUESTION 75
Which of the following methods is called first in an Activity when another activity gets into the foreground?

A. onStop( )
B. onPause( ) C. onDestroy( ) D. onExit( )

Correct Answer: B Section: (none) Explanation

Explanation/Reference:

QUESTION 76
Which of the following attributes of the activity tag in the manifest file is used to set an activity screen to landscape orientation?

A. screenorientation = landscape
B. screenOrientation="landscape"
C. android:ScreenOrientation="landscape" D. android:screenOrientation="landscape"

Correct Answer: D Section: (none) Explanation

Explanation/Reference:

QUESTION 77
What is NOT true about the AndroidManifest.xml file?

A. It declares the views used within the application.
B. It declares user permissions the application requires. C. It declares application components.

D. It declares hardware and software features used within the application.

Correct Answer: A **Section: (none) Explanation**

Explanation/Reference:

QUESTION 78
If your application is throwing exception android.content.ActivityNotFoundException, which of the following could resolve the problem?

A. Create a new sub-class of the View class
B. Create a new broadcast receiver
C. Create the activity layout
D. Add the activity to AndroidManifest.xml

Correct Answer: D **Section: (none) Explanation**

Explanation/Reference:

QUESTION 79
Consider the following code:

```
Intent intent = new Intent();
intent.setAction(Intent.ACTION_VIEW);
intent.setData(android.net.Uri.parse("http://www.androidatc.com"
)); startActivity(intent);
```

Which of the following is correct about the code above? A. It

sends a result to a new Activity in a Bundle.
B. It will not compile without adding the INTERNET permission the Manifest file.
C. It starts any activity in the application that has a WebView in its layout.
D. When it is executed, the system starts an intent resolution process to start the right Activity.

Correct Answer: D **Section: (none) Explanation**

Explanation/Reference:

QUESTION 80
Which of the following is NOT true about <activity> tag in AndroidManifest file?

A. Declares an activity that implements part of the application's visual user interface. B. Contained in <application> tag.
C. Declares a single hardware or software feature that is used by the application.
D. Has an attribute that specifies the name of the Activity sub-class that implements the activity.

Correct Answer: C Section: (none) Explanation

Explanation/Reference:

QUESTION 81
Which of the following Android View sub-classes uses the WebKit rendering engine to display web pages?

A. PageView
B. WebView

C. MapView
D. HttpClient

Correct Answer: B Section: (none) Explanation

Explanation/Reference:

QUESTION 82
Which of the following lines of codes adds zoom controls to a WebView?

A. webView.getSettings().setBuiltInZoomControls(true); B. webView.getSettings().setZoomControls(true);
C.
webView.getZoomSettings().setControls(CONTROLS.enabled);
D. Zoom controls are included by default in WebViews

Correct Answer: A Section: (none) Explanation

Explanation/Reference:

QUESTION 83
Which of the following best explains the Android option menus?

A. It is a popup menu that displays a list of items in a vertical list anchored to the view that invoked the menu.
B. It is a floating menu that appears when the user performs a long-click on an element. It provides actions that affect the selected content or context frame.
C. It is the primary collection of menu items for an activity where you should place actions that have a global impact on the app, such as "Search," "Compose email," and "Settings."
D. It is a type of List Activity with predefined headers and footers for special commands.

Correct Answer: C Section: (none) Explanation

Explanation/Reference:

QUESTION 84
Which of the following best explains the Android context menus?

A. It is a popup menu displays a list of items in a vertical list that's anchored to the view that invoked the menu.
B. It is a floating menu that appears when the user performs a long-click on an element. It provides actions that affect the selected content or context frame.
C. It is the primary collection of menu items for an activity. It's where you should place actions that have a global impact on the app, such as "Search," "Compose email," and "Settings".
D. It is a sub-menu of an options menu item.

Correct Answer: B Section: (none) Explanation

Explanation/Reference:

QUESTION 85
Consider the following code :
@Override

```
public void onCreateContextMenu(ContextMenu menu, View v,
        ContextMenuInfo menuInfo) {
    super.onCreateContextMenu(menu, v, menuInfo);
    menu.setHeaderTitle("Menu");
    AdapterContextMenuInfo cmi = (AdapterContextMenuInfo)
    menuInfo;
    menu.add(1, cmi.position, 0, "Open file");
    menu.add(2, cmi.position, 0, "Save file");
}
```

Which of the following best explains the code above? A. The

code inflates an xml file into menu items.
B. The code creates menu items for context menu
programmatically.
C. The code assign actions to menu items.
D. The code opens a menu resource file, modifies it, and saves
the changes.

Correct Answer: B Section: (none) Explanation

Explanation/Reference:

QUESTION 86
Which of the following applies a context menu on a ListView?
(Choose two)

A. ListView lv = getListView();
lv.registerForContextMenu()
B. ListView lv= getListView();
registerForContextMenu(lv);
C. ListView lv = (ListView) findViewById(R.id.list_view_id);
registerForContextMenu(lv)
D. getListView().setConextMenuEnabled(true)

Correct Answer: BC Section: (none) Explanation

Explanation/Reference:

QUESTION 87
Which of the following methods updates a ListView when an
element is added to the data set?

A. notify( )
B. notifyAll( )
C. notifyDataSetChanged( )
D. notifyDataSetInvalidate( )

Correct Answer: C Section: (none) Explanation
Explanation/Reference:

QUESTION 88
The values of which of the following classes cannot be mapped in a Bundle object?

A. Parcelable objects B. Primitive data types C. Serializable objects D. Context

Correct Answer: D Section: (none) Explanation

Explanation/Reference:

QUESTION 89
Which of the following is true about method startActivity?

A. It starts a new activity and destroys the previous one. B. It starts a new activity and sends it to the foreground. C. It starts a new activity and resumes the previous one. D. It starts a new activity in a paused mode.

Correct Answer: B Section: (none) Explanation

Explanation/Reference:

QUESTION 90
Which of the following are primary pieces of information that are required to define in an implicit Intent?

A. An action to be performed and data to operate on.
B. An action to be performed and a category for additional information. C. A Bundle for extra data.

D. A category of additional information and data to operate on.

QUESTION 91
When is the intent resolution process triggered?

A. When the system receives an implicit intent to start an activity.
B. When an explicit intent starts a service.
C. When the system receives an explicit intent to start an activity.
D. When the application calls method startAcitivyIntentResolution.

Correct Answer: A **Section: (none) Explanation**

Explanation/Reference:

QUESTION 92
Which of the following applies to the onDraw( ) method of class View? (Choose two)

A. It must be overridden if a customized drawing of a view is required. B. It takes two parameters: a Canvas and a View.
C. It takes one parameter of type Canvas.
D. It uses the Canvas parameter to draw the border of the activity that contains it.

Correct Answer: AC **Section: (none) Explanation**

Explanation/Reference: QUESTION 93

Which of the following you cannot achieve by creating your own View sub-classes?

A. Create a completely new customized View type.
B. Combine a group of View components into a new single component. C. Specify when to destroy an activity and all its views.

D. Override the way that an existing component is displayed on the screen.

Correct Answer: C **Section: (none) Explanation**

Explanation/Reference:

QUESTION 94
Which of the following is required to allow Android Studio to interact with a custom view?

A. Provide a constructor that takes a Context and an AttributeSet object as parameters. B. Provide a constructor that takes a Context object as parameter.
C. Extend class View.
D. Override method onDraw() of class View.

Correct Answer: A **Section: (none) Explanation**

Explanation/Reference:

QUESTION 95
What are the main two types of threads in Android?

A. Main thread and worker threads. B. Main thread and UI thread.
C. Activities and services.
D. Main thread and background process.

Correct Answer: A
Section: (none)
Explanation

Explanation/Reference:

QUESTION 96
Whic of the following AsyncTask methods is NOT executed on the UI thread?

A. onPreExecute( ) B. onPostExecute( ) C. publishProgress( )

D. onProgressUpdate( )

Correct Answer: C Section: (none) Explanation

Explanation/Reference:

QUESTION 97
Which of the following is NOT true about method getWindow() of class Dialog?

A. It retrieves the current window for the activity.
B. It can be used to access parts of the Windows API. C. It displays the dialog on the screen.
D. It returns null if the activity is not visible.

Correct Answer: C Section: (none) Explanation

Explanation/Reference:

QUESTION 98
Which of the following is a NOT valid form of notification invoked by the NotificationManager?

A. A Flashing LED.

B. A persistent icon in the status bar. C. A sound played.
D. A SMS sent.

Correct Answer: D Section: (none) Explanation

Explanation/Reference:

QUESTION 99
Which of the following is true about the Dialog class? (Choose two)

A. You can add a custom layout to a dialog using setContentView( ). B. A dialog has a life-cycle independent of the Activity.
C. A dialog is displayed on the screen using method show( ).

D. It does not have a method to access the activity that owns it.

Correct Answer: AC Section: (none) Explanation

Explanation/Reference:

QUESTION 100
Which of the following is mandatory for a Notification object to contain? (Choose three)

A. A small icon
B. A detail text.
C. A notification sound
D. A title

Correct Answer: ABD Section: (none) Explanation

Explanation/Reference:

QUESTION 101
What is the location of the APK generated by the build system of Android Studio?

A. app/build/apk
B. app/apks
C. app/build/outputs/apk
D. app/intermediates/outputs/apk

Correct Answer: C Section: (none) Explanation

Explanation/Reference:

QUESTION 102
Which of the following best explains the Android popup menus?

A. It is only displayed when the user presses the home button twice.
B. It displays a list of items vertically and is anchored to the view that invoked the menu.

C. It is a floating menu that appears when the user performs a long-click on an element.
D. It is the primary collection of menu items for an activity. It's where you should place actions that have a global impact on the app, such as "Search", "Compose email", and "Settings".

Correct Answer: B Section: (none) Explanation

Explanation/Reference: QUESTION 103

Which of the following best defines an Android fragment?

A. It is a portion of the user-interface that is embedded in an activity.
B. It is the component that allows asynchronous loading of data into an activity.
C. It is an XML file that defines the layout of an activity.
D. It is a type of a drawable resource file.

Correct Answer: A Section: (none) Explanation

Explanation/Reference:

QUESTION 104
Which of the following statements is NOT correct about Android fragments?

A. Multiple fragments can be combined in a single activity.
B. The life-cycle of a fragment is totally independent of the activity hosting it.
C. Fragments have their own life-cycle.
D. You can add/remove fragments to and an activity dynamically; i.e. while the activity is running.

Correct Answer: B Section: (none) Explanation

Explanation/Reference:

QUESTION 105

Which of the following are benefits for using fragments in your application? (Choose Two)

A. Simplify the reusability of UI components.
B. Build different layouts for different device configurations.
C. Add an action bar to your application.
D. Dynamically add and remove UI components to an activity.

Correct Answer: AD
Section: (none)
Explanation

Explanation/Reference:

QUESTION 106
What is the Android SDK version required for best performance of "Instant Run" feature of Android Studio?

A. 19 and above
B. 20 and above
C. 15 and above
D. 21 and above

Correct Answer: D Section: (none) Explanation

Explanation/Reference:

QUESTION 107
In which of the following windows (inside Android studio) can you check the performance profiling information of your app?

A. Monitors
B. Watches
C. Debug
D. Preview

Correct Answer: A Section: (none) Explanation

Explanation/Reference:

QUESTION 108
Which of the following is NOT the built-in layout manager provided by RecyclerView?

A. LinearLayoutManager

B. RelativeLayoutManager
C. GridLayoutManager
D. StaggeredGridLayoutManager

Correct Answer: B Section: (none) Explanation

Explanation/Reference:

QUESTION 109
Which of the following measurement units are used in coordinate system when adding locations for testing via Emulator tools? (Choose two)

A. Hexadecimal
B. Meters
C. Decimal
D. Sexagesimal

Correct Answer: CD Section: (none) Explanation

Explanation/Reference:

QUESTION 110
Which of the following is NOT correct about CardView?

A. Views can be added inside CardView .
B. CardView is available through support library.
C. Views cannot be added inside CardView .
D. It is used to make card-like views .

Correct Answer: C Section: (none) Explanation

Explanation/Reference:

QUESTION 111
Which of the following features CANNOT be controlled through CardView's properties?

A. Shadow
B. Corner
C. Elevation
D. Depth

Correct Answer: D Section: (none) Explanation

Explanation/Reference:

QUESTION 112
Which of the following is correct about Runtime permissions?

A. These are granted while app is running on device. B. These are granted at the time of installation.
C. These can be revoked or canceled at any time resulting in cancelling all the permissions of the app.
D. Runtime Permissions are added below the normal permissions in AndroidManifest.xml with the tag <uses-runtime-permission/>.

Correct Answer: A Section: (none) Explanation

Explanation/Reference:

QUESTION 113
Which of the following is added as intent action for deep linking?

A. ACTION_VIEW
B. ACTION_BROWSE
C. ACTION_URL
D. ACTION_SEARCH

Correct Answer: A Section: (none) Explanation

Explanation/Reference:

QUESTION 114
Which of the following are NOT correct about Normal Permissions? (Choose two)

A. They have low level impact on privacy of users.
B. They do not impact the privacy of users.
C. You have to get them approved explicitly from user at runtime.
D. ACCESS_WIFI_STATE is classified as normal permission.

Correct Answer: AC Section: (none) Explanation

Explanation/Reference:

QUESTION 115
android:scheme is added in which of the following tags?

A. <action>
B. <data>
C. <category>
D. <url>

Correct Answer: B Section: (none) Explanation

Explanation/Reference:

QUESTION 116
How many constraint handles are available to us as part of the ConstraintLayout?

A. Review Handle, Sides Handle.
B. Rescope Handle, Edges Constraint Handle, Centre Constraint Handle.
C. Resize Handle, Side Constraint Handle, Baseline Constraint Handle.
D. All answers are incorrect.

Correct Answer: C Section: (none) Explanation

Explanation/Reference:

QUESTION 117
Which of the following is a valid attribute of ConstraintLayout?

A. layout_constraintEdge_toEdgeOf
B. layout_constraintMiddle_toMiddleOf
C. layout_constraintLeft_toRightOf
D. All answers are correct

Correct Answer: C Section: (none) Explanation

Explanation/Reference:

QUESTION 118
In order to perform a shared element transition, we need to :

A. Specify the same android:id attribute to the 2 views (shared views) in both the entry/exit pair of activities. Both the shared views can be of different View types. B. Specify the same android:id attribute to the 2 views (shared views) in both the entry/exit pair of activities. Both the shared views should be of the same View
types.
C. Specify the same android:transitionName attribute to the 2 views (shared views) in both the entry/exit pair of activities. Both the shared views should be of the same View types.
D. Specify the same android:sharedTransition attribute to the 2 views (shared views) in both the entry/exit pair of activities. Both the shared views should be of the different View types.

Correct Answer: C Section: (none) Explanation

Explanation/Reference:

QUESTION 119
What code would you need to use for a reverse transition when going from the second activity, back to the first?

A. finish(true) B. finish( )
C. finishTransition( )

D. All answers are incorrect

Correct Answer: D Section: (none) Explanation

Explanation/Reference:

QUESTION 120
Which of the following are the possible values of app:fabSize attribute of FloatingActionButton?

A. small, normal
B. mini, normal, default
C. auto, mini, normal
D. small, medium, large

Correct Answer: C Section: (none) Explanation
Explanation/Reference:

QUESTION 121
Which attribute would you use to animate the FloatingActionButton, moving it "into" the screen when user clicks it?

A. app:pressedTranslationZ B. app:ZTranslation
C. app:ZClickTranslation
D. app:pressedTranslation

Correct Answer: A Section: (none) Explanation

Explanation/Reference:

QUESTION 122
Which of the following methods invoke a Snackbar?

A. Make( ); B. View( ); C. Show( );
D. Create( );

Correct Answer: C Section: (none) Explanation

Explanation/Reference:

QUESTION 123
Which of the following methods defines a Snackbar view?

A. Make( )
B. View( );
C. Show( )
D. Create( );

Correct Answer: Section: (none) Explanation

Explanation/Reference:

QUESTION 124
On which of the following thread does a Service run?

A. Background Thread
B. Intent Thread
C. Main Thread
D. System Thread

Correct Answer: C Section: (none) Explanation

Explanation/Reference:

QUESTION 125
Which parameters does the system pass to method onReceive( )
of BroadcastReceiver ?

A. Context
B. View and Intent
C. Context and Intent
D. Activity and Context

Correct Answer: C Section: (none) Explanation

Explanation/Reference: QUESTION 126

Which of the following methods are invoked when a Broadcast
Receiver receives a message?

A. onReceive( ) B. onMessage( ) C. onArrival( )
D. onBind( )

Correct Answer: A **Section: (none) Explanation**

Explanation/Reference:

QUESTION 127
Which ORMLite library annotation would you use to mark a class
Xyz to be persisted in SQL database?

A. @DatabaseClass
B. @DatabaseTable(tableName = "xyz") C.
@DataTable(tableName = "xyz")
D. @PersistenceTable(name = "xyz")

Correct Answer: B **Section: (none) Explanation**

Explanation/Reference:

QUESTION 128
Which of the following statements hold true about persisting data
types using ORMLite third party library?

A. All persisted classes must define a no-argument constructor
which must have at least package level visibility.
B. All persisted classes must define a one-argument constructor,
which takes the name of the table as its argument. The
constructor is required to have private level visibility.
C. All persisted classes must define a one-argument constructor,
which takes the name of the table as its argument. The
constructor is required to have public level visibility.
D. All answers are incorrect.
Correct Answer: A **Section: (none) Explanation**

Explanation/Reference:

QUESTION 129
Custom views for notifications are allowed in Android.

A. True. B. False.
C. Depends on the device manufacturer. D. Depends on developer skills.

Correct Answer: A Section: (none) Explanation

Explanation/Reference:

QUESTION 130
Which of the following Classes is responsible for capturing the location using GPS?
A. GPSLocationManager
B. GPSManager
C. LocationManager
D. GPS Provider

Correct Answer: C Section: (none) Explanation
Explanation/Reference:

QUESTION 131
Capturing GPS coordinates require creating a project on Google console and enable GPS Capturing.

A. True B. False C.
D.

Correct Answer: B Section: (none) Explanation

Explanation/Reference:

QUESTION 132
Which of the following permissions is not required to integrate Google Maps into your Android application?

A. android.permission.WRITE_EXTERNAL_STORAGE
B. android.permission.READ_EXTERNAL_STORAGE
C. android.permission.ACCESS_FINE_LOCATION
D. All answers are correct

Correct Answer: C Section: (none) Explanation

QUESTION 133
Which of the following statements is true about Google Map API key?

A. Google Map API key is unique per Developer.

B. Google Map API key is unique per Project.

C. Google Map API key is unique per User.

D. Google Map API key is unique per Device.

Correct Answer: B Section: (none) Explanation

Explanation/Reference:

QUESTION 134
Which of the following functions is used to add pins to Google Maps?

A. locatePin(MarkerOptions)
B. attachMarker(MarkerOptions)
C. attachPin(MarkerOptions)
D. addMarker(MarkerOptions)

Correct Answer: D Section: (none) Explanation

Explanation/Reference:

QUESTION 135
Which of the following interfaces is necessary to access Google Maps once it is ready?

A. OnMapReadyCallback
B. OnMapReady
C. OnGoogleMapReadyCallback
D. OnGoogleMapReady

Correct Answer: A Section: (none) Explanation

Explanation/Reference: QUESTION 136

Which of these is NOT recommended in the Android Developer's Guide as a method of creating an individual View?

A. Create it by extending the android.view.View class
B. Create it by extending already existing View classes such as Button or TextView
C. Create it by copying the source of an already existing View class such as Button or TextView
D. Create it by combining multiple Views

Correct Answer: C Section: (none) Explanation

Explanation/Reference:

QUESTION 137
Which of these is the incorrect explanation of the Android SDK and AVD Manager?

A. They are provided from version 1.6 of the SDK. Up to Version 1.5, there was an AVD Manager but it lacked SDK management functions.
B. You can create and startup AVD, and on startup you can delete user data up to that point.
C. The "android" command can be used if "<SDK install folder>/tools" is added to the command path.
D. The development tools that can be downloaded from Android SDK and AVD Manager are SDK Android platform, NDK-platform, emulator images, and USB
                    drivers for handsets.

Correct Answer: D Section: (none) Explanation

Explanation/Reference:

QUESTION 138
Which of these is the correct explanation regarding the following methods? (1)android.content.Context.sendBroadcast (2)android.content.Context.startActivity

A. Both methods are defined by overloading. B. Both methods throw an exception.

C. Both methods are asynchronous.
D. Both methods are able to broadcast an Intent.

Correct Answer: D Section: (none) Explanation

Explanation/Reference:

QUESTION 139
Which of the following is incorrect about ProgressDialog?

A. ProgressDialog inherits from the AlertDialog class.
B. ProgressDialog can be set as 2 types of style:
STYLE_HORIZONTAL and STYLE_SPINNER.
C. ProgressDialog is able to apply a custom XML-defined layout
by using the setContentView(...) method.
D. ProgressDialog can be freely configured to use a Drawable
class to display as its progress bar.

Correct Answer: C Section: (none) Explanation

Explanation/Reference:

QUESTION 140
Which of these is the correct function of Traceview?

A. Displays a graphical task execution log.
B. Displays graphically a memory acquisition and release log.
C. Displays graphically the call stack.
D. Displays graphically the UI state hierarchy.

Correct Answer: A Section: (none) Explanation

Explanation/Reference:

QUESTION 141
Which of the following is the correct way to add access
permission to your application?

A. Add a <uses-permission> tag as a child tag of the <manifest> tag in AndroidManifest.xml. B. Add a <add-permission> tag as a child tag of the <manifest> tag in AndroidManifest.xml.
C. Add a <uses-permission> tag as a child tag of the <application> tag in AndroidManifest.xml. D. add a <permission> tag as a child tag of the <application> tag in AndroidManifest.xml.

Correct Answer: A Section: (none) Explanation

Explanation/Reference:

QUESTION 142
When including a text file in your application to read from as a resource, what is the recommended location of such file?

A. res/anim B. res/files C. res/raw
D. res/values

Correct Answer: C Section: (none) Explanation

Explanation/Reference:

QUESTION 143
Which of the following statements is correct about SQLite? (Choose Two)
A. It is an object-relational database.
B. It is a client-server format.
C. It is possible to create and access a database by using SQLOpenHelper.
D. It can be accessed by other applications through ContentProvider.

Correct Answer: CD Section: (none) Explanation

Explanation/Reference:

QUESTION 144
Which of the following statements is incorrect about Android Device Monitor in Android Studio?

A. You can display a list of currently running threads and select one to check its stack trace.
B. It can add dynamically Google SDK libraries to the Android image running on the emulator. C. You can forcibly execute garbage collection and check the present heap usage status.
D. You can do simulations of network zone speed and bandwidth limitations.

Correct Answer: B Section: (none) Explanation

Explanation/Reference:

QUESTION 145
Which of the following is incorrect about intents?

A. They can be used to start an Activity.
B. They can be used to start a service.
C. They can be used to start database insertion.
D. They can be used to start a dialog-themed activity.

Correct Answer: C Section: (none) Explanation

Explanation/Reference:

QUESTION 146
Method onDraw() of class android.view.View has the following signature:

A. public void onDraw(Color)
B. public void onDraw(Canvas)
C. public boolean onDraw(Canvas) D. public Canvas onDraw( )

Correct Answer: B Section: (none) Explanation

Explanation/Reference:

QUESTION 147
To create a blank Wear activity in Android Studio, the project should have a minimum SDK version >= 20.

A. True
B. False

Correct Answer: A Section: (none) Explanation

Explanation/Reference:

QUESTION 148
When publishing an update to your application to the market, the following must be taken into consideration:

A. The package name must be the same, but the .apk may be signed with a different private key.
B. The package name does not have to be the same and the .apk can be signed with a different private key.
C. The package name must be the same and the .apk must be signed with the same private key.
D. The package name does not have to be the same, but the .apk must be signed with the same private key.

Correct Answer: C
Section: (none)
Explanation

Explanation/Reference:

QUESTION 149
Which of these is the incorrect method for an Application to save local data?

A. Extend PreferencesActivity and save in an XML file.
B. Save as a file in the local file system.
C. Save in the database using SQLite.
D. Save in the hash table file using the Dictionary class.

Correct Answer: D Section: (none) Explanation

Explanation/Reference:

QUESTION 150
Which UI does the following code builds?

<?xml version="1.0" encoding="utf-8"?>

```
<LinearLayout
xmlns:android=http://schemas.android.com/apk/res/android
android:layout_width="match_parent"
android:layout_height="match_parent"
android:orientation="vertical" >
<LinearLayout android:layout_width="match_parent"
android:layout_height="wrap_content"
android:orientation="horizontal" >
<TextView android:id="@+id/textView1"
android:layout_width="wrap_content"
android:layout_height="wrap_content" android:text="Name:" />
<EditText android:id="@+id/editText1"
android:layout_width="match_parent"
android:layout_height="wrap_content"
android:layout_weight="1" android:ems="10" />
</LinearLayout>
<Button android:id="@+id/button1"
android:layout_width="wrap_content"
android:layout_height="wrap_content" android:text="Post" />
</LinearLayout>
```

A. An edit text to the left of a text view and a button beneath it.

B. An edit text to the right of a text view and a button to the right of the text view.

C. An edit text to the right of a text view and a button beneath them.

D. A text view, an edit text beneath it and the button beneath the edit text.]

Correct Answer: C **Section: (none) Explanation**

Explanation/Reference:

QUESTION 151
Consider the following code:
Intent i = new Intent(this, MainActivity.class);
i.addFlags(Intent.FLAG_ACTIVITY_CLEAR_TOP);
startActivity(i);
What best explains the code above?

A. The activity being launched is already running in the current task, then instead of launching a new instance of that activity, all of the other activities on top of it will be closed and this Intent will be delivered to the (now on top) old activity as a new Intent.

B. Any existing task that would be associated with the activity to be cleared before the activity is started.
C. A new Activity will be launched and it will be on the top of the stack.
D. A new activity will be launched but will be in full-screen mode.

Correct Answer: A Section: (none) Explanation

Explanation/Reference:

QUESTION 152
Which of the following lines of code is used to pass a value to the next activity?

A. Intent i = new Intent(this,newActivity);
i.addExtra("test");
startActivity(i);
B. Intent i = new Intent(this,newActivity);
i.putValue("test");
startActivity(i);
C. Intent i = new Intent(this,newActivity);
i.putValue("value1","test"); startActivity(i);
D. Intent i = new Intent(this,newActivity);
i.putExtra("value1","test"); startActivity(i);

Correct Answer: D Section: (none) Explanation

Explanation/Reference:

QUESTION 153
Consider the following AndroidManifest.xml file.

```
<?xml version="1.0" encoding="utf-8"?>
<manifest
xmlns:android="http://schemas.android.com/apk/res/android"
package="com.androidatc "
android:versionCode="1"
android:versionName="1.0" >
<uses-sdk android:minSdkVersion="12"
android:targetSdkVersion="17" />
<application android:name="MyApp " android:allowBackup="true"
android:icon="@drawable/ic_launcher"
android:label="@string/app_name"
```

```
    android:theme="@style/AppTheme" >
<activity android:name="com.androidatc.MainActivity"
    android:label="@string/app_name"
    android:screenOrientation="portrait" >
    <intent-filter>
    <action android:name="android.intent.action.MAIN" />
    <category android:name="android.intent.category.LAUNCHER"
    />
    </intent-filter>
    </activity>
    <uses-permission
    android:name="android.permission.INTERNET" />
    </application>
    </manifest>
```

Which of the following is correct?

A. The application will run as intended.
B. The application will not compile.
C. The application will crash on fetching data from the internet.
D. The app will run in Landscape orientation.

Correct Answer: B **Section: (none) Explanation**

Explanation/Reference:

QUESTION 154
Consider the following AndroidManifest.xml file:

```
<?xml version="1.0" encoding="utf-8"?>
<manifest
xmlns:android="http://schemas.android.com/apk/res/android"
package="com.androidatc.test"
android:versionCode="1" android:versionName="1.0" >

<uses-sdk android:minSdkVersion="8"
    android:targetSdkVersion="17" />
<application android:icon="@drawable/ic_launcher"
    android:label="@string/app_name"
    android:theme="@android:style/Theme.Light.NoTitleBar" >

<activity android:screenOrientation="portrait"
    android:label="@string/app_name" >
                            <intent-filter>
```

```xml
<action android:name="android.intent.action.MAIN" />
<category android:name="android.intent.category.LAUNCHER"
/>
                    </intent-filter>
                    </activity>
</application>
<uses-permission
android:name="android.permission.INTERNET"></uses-
permission>
<activity  android:name=".Compute"
android:screenOrientation="portrait" />
</manifest>
```

What is the syntax error of this file?

A. The INTERNET permission must be removed.
B. Tag uses-sdk must have attribute android:maxSdkVersion
set.
C. The activity under <application> tag should have the
android:name property.
D. The <activity> tag for Activity ".Compute" should be contained
inside <application> tag.

Correct Answer: D Section: (none) Explanation

Explanation/Reference:

QUESTION 155
Which of the following lines of code sets the entire Activity
window as a WebView?

A. WebView webview = new WebView(this);
webview.setAsWindow;
B. setContentView(R.layout.webview);
C. WebView webview = new WebView(this);
setContentView(webview);

D. setContentView("http://www.androidatc.com");

Correct Answer: C Section: (none) Explanation

Explanation/Reference:

QUESTION 156
Consider the following the code :

```
public boolean onCreateOptionsMenu(Menu menu) { MenuInflater
    inflater = getMenuInflater(); inflater.inflate(R.menu.game_menu,
    menu);
                            return true;
}
```

Which of the following is true about the code above?

A. The code is auto generated and should not be edited.
B. This method handles clicks and assign actions to menu items.
C. This function inflates an XML file in the res/menu folder into
menu items.
D. This method inflates an XML file in the res/layout folder into
layout.

Correct Answer: C Section: (none) Explanation

Explanation/Reference:

QUESTION 157
Consider the following :

```
<?xml version="1.0" encoding="utf-8"?>
<menu
    xmlns:android="http://schemas.android.com/apk/res/android">
<item android:id="@+id/create_new" android:title="@string/create_new"
    />
<item android:id="@+id/open" android:title="@string/open" />
        </menu>
            public boolean onOptionsItemSelected(MenuItem item) {
                    switch (item.getItemId()) {
                        case R.id.create_new:
        newFile();
            return true default:
        return super.onOptionsItemSelected(item);
        }
}
```

Upon clicking on one of the menu items, the application did not
behave as intended. Which of the following might be the cause of
this problem? (Choose two)

A. The developer did not set onClickListener on the menu item.

B. The developer did not include "R.id.open" in the switch case.

C. The developer should create onOptionsItemSelected method for each menu item.

D. The developer did not override the activity method "onCreateOptionsMenu" and enflate the given menu layout.

Correct Answer: BD Section: (none) Explanation

Explanation/Reference:

QUESTION 158
Which of the following is not true about using a WebView in your application?

A. You can retrieve WebSettings with getSettings(), then enable/disable JavaScript.

B. You need to add permission "android.permission.ACCESS_NETWORK_STATE".

C. You use loadURL to load a webpage.

D. You use loadData to load HTML.

Correct Answer: B
Section: (none)
Explanation

Explanation/Reference:

QUESTION 159
Which of the following is NOT true about class ListActivity?

A. An activity that displays a list of items by binding to a data set.

B. Its layout must be set by calling method setContentView inside onCreate.

C. It contains a ListView object that can be bound to different data sets.

D. A data source that can be bound in a ListActivity can be an array or Cursor holding query results.

Correct Answer: B Section: (none) Explanation

QUESTION 160
Which of the following is true about this code snippet? (Choose two)

```
Intent intent = new
Intent(Intent.ACTION_DIAL,Uri.parse("tel:555-1234"));
startActivity(intent);
```

A. This is an explicit intent that start the system's dialer.
B. The system will pass the number to the dialer without using permission CALL_PHONE.
C. The system will perform an intent resolution to start the proper activity.
D. The code will not compile.

Correct Answer: BC Section: (none) Explanation

Explanation/Reference:

QUESTION 161
Which of the following is NOT true about class AsyncTask?

A. It must be used by sub-classing it.
B. It must be created on the UI thread.
C. Its sub-class override at least two methods: doInBackground, onPostExecute.
D. It uses three generic types.

Correct Answer: C Section: (none) Explanation

Explanation/Reference:

QUESTION 162
Which of the following is a rule that developers must always follow when writing multi-threaded Android applications? (Choose two)

A. A worker thread must not be created from inside the UI thread.

B. Each UI thread must not create more than one worker thread.

C. The UI thread must never be blocked.

D. The Android UI must not be accessed from outside the UI thread.

Correct Answer: CD Section: (none) Explanation

Explanation/Reference:

QUESTION 163
Which of the following are layout-related methods called by the framework on views, and you can override them when customizing a view? (Choose two)

A. onMeasure( )
B. onDraw( )
C. onKeyUp( )
D. onSizeChanged( )

Correct Answer: AD Section: (none) Explanation

Explanation/Reference:

QUESTION 164
What does the following line of code do?

```
Toast toast = Toast.makeText(this,"Android ATC",
Toast.LENGTH_LONG);
toast.setGravity(Gravity.TOP|Gravity.RIGHT, 0, 0);
toast.show( );
```

A. The toast will have its UI components place on the top-right corner.

B. The toast will appear on the top-right corner.

C. The toast will show the text message on top-right corner of the toast box.

D. The toast will appear at the center of the screen at position (0,0), but aligned to the top-right corner.

Correct Answer: B **Section: (none) Explanation**

Explanation/Reference:

QUESTION 165
Which of the following is NOT true about a content provider?

A. It manages access to structured data.
B. It cannot be used from inside an Activity.
C. It facilitates access to Android's SQLite databases.
D. To access data in it, method getContentResolver() of the application's Context is used.

Correct Answer: B **Section: (none) Explanation**

Explanation/Reference:

QUESTION 166
Which of the following is NOT true about SQLiteOpenHelper class? (Choose two)

A. It has two abstract methods: onCreate( ) and onUpgrade( ).
B. It is used to perform database querying.
C. It manages database creation and updates.
D. It manages database versions using ContentProvider.

Correct Answer: BD **Section: (none) Explanation**

Explanation/Reference:

QUESTION 167
Which of the following is correct dependency for adding CardView?

A. dependencies {compile 'com.android.support:cardview-v7:24.2.1' }

B. dependencies {compile 'com.android.support:CardView-v7:24.2.1' }

C. dependencies {compile 'com.android.support:cardView-v7:24.2.1' }

D. dependencies {compile 'com.android.support.cardview-v7:24.2.1' }

Correct Answer: A Section: (none) Explanation

Explanation/Reference:

QUESTION 168
Which of the following is the correct syntax for adding CardView to a layout file?

A. <android.support.v7.widget.cardview ... /> B.
C.
D.

Correct Answer: B Section: (none) Explanation

.

www.ingramcontent.com/pod-product-compliance
Lightning Source LLC
LaVergne TN
LVHW052314060326
832902LV00021B/3882